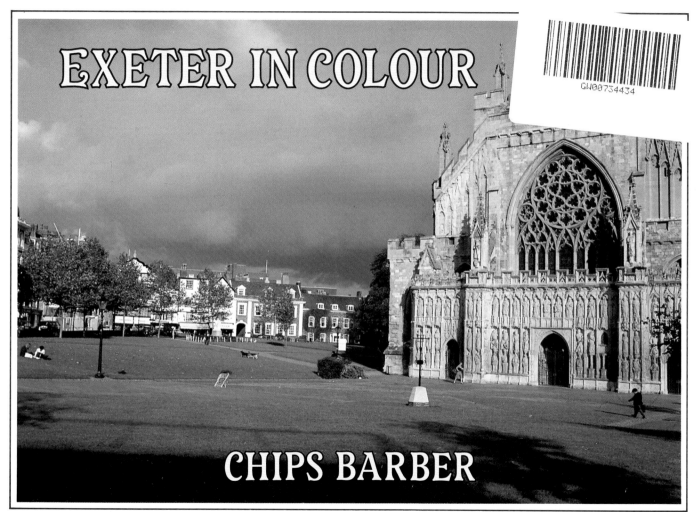

EXETER IN COLOUR

CHIPS BARBER

The River Exe

The River Exe rises high on Exmoor but the river doesn't only give its name to the moor in Somerset it also gives its name to the City of Exeter in the heart of Glorious Devon. On its travels it flows through rolling countryside, past beautiful settlements and under many attractive ancient stone bridges. This is Bickleigh and the bridge is believed to be the one which inspired Paul Simon to write his memorable song "Bridge Over Troubled Waters". From here the Exe wends its way on towards Exeter and increases in volume, as it approaches the city, with tributaries like the Culm and Creedy adding to its flow.

Exeter's First Stone Bridge

A thousand years ago the River Exe was tidal up to this bridge. It was not constrained within man made banks as it is today and was therefore wider but shallower. Although it was possible to wade across the river then, this was always a precarious activity particularly after heavy rain. About 1231 it was deemed necessary to construct a bridge to cross these 'troubled waters' and Walter Gervase, who at that time was Mayor of Exeter, was largely instrumental in this. However it was many years before it was started—the foundations were not laid until 1257—and poor Gervase did not live to see his bridge finished as he died in 1259 when the bridge was at an advanced stage. Some people believed that he was actually buried in the bridge because, many centuries later, the skeleton of a tall man was exhumed in 1883 when part of the bridge was taken down.

The House that Moved

Opposite are two well known Exeter landmarks, The House that Moved (far left) and Stepcote Hill. The former is so named as originally it stood a few hundred yards down the road but a road widening scheme was destined to go right through it. Very cleverly it dodged demolition by running up the hill! In the other picture it can be seen in its present location beside the West Gate and opposite St Mary Steps Church. Stepcote Hill descends to this point immediately to the right of the church and until about 1778 it was the main route in from the west. But the building of a new bridge over the Exe leading into New Bridge Street meant that visitors had a less arduous journey to the city.

The Custom House

On this site, in the corner of Exeter Quay, is reputedly the first brick building in Exeter which dates back to 1681. Originally the arches at the front were open, giving it a totally different appearance. It is listed as an ancient monument and is a reminder that Exeter was once a thriving port, specially in the days of the woollen trade. Inside the Custom House are some marvellous ornamental plaster ceilings, the work of a craftsman called John Abbot who came from the quiet backwater settlement of Frithelstock in Northwest Devon. Outside, mounted on two gun carriages, are cannons which arrived at Exeter Quay in 1819 en route to the Wellington Monument in Somerset, but because of a dispute over landing fees never left. For many years they were used as iron bollards further along the quay but were moved to their present position when the area began to develop as a tourist attraction.

6

A Bridge over the River Exe

The River Exe wends its way between man made banks and beneath man made bridges as it approaches Exeter Quay. In the recent past much has happened to the Exe as it passes Exeter. For many years, 1960 in particular, severe flooding caused so much damage that an elaborate flood prevention scheme was constructed to alleviate the watery problem. It is unlikely that this bridge will ever be washed away by floods and should afford a safe and dry crossing to Haven Banks for many years to come.

The Swanee River?

The waterside near Exeter Quay is a popular spot for local people to feed the swans and other small birds which congregate here. These swans certainly know when it is feeding time!

In the 1970s the BBC used Exeter for filming the television serial "The Onedin Line". Thus 20th century Exeter became 19th century Liverpool as the original settlement was not authentic enough! With various embellishments the main warehouses on the Quay provided a suitable backcloth. Throughout the two series of 50 episodes, Exeter or Bayards Cove at Dartmouth continually featured—often in the same scene! It was quite common to see the "Charlotte Rhodes" sail straight off from Exeter Quay down the Dart Estuary—such is the magic and trickery of film makers. There was a lapse of several years between the two series and, in the meantime, the motorway bridge was built across the Exe Estuary near Topsham. This caused several headaches and necessitated that the tall masted ships, used in the series, had to be demasted and then remasted. The building of a new Exe Bridge upstream also kept the film makers on their toes as the noise was extreme at times. My book "Made in Devon" gives a more detailed insight to the making of this and other television programmes and films made in Devon—and is full of bizarre and amusing anecdotes.

The Prospect Inn on the Quay (which incidentally was also used for some indoor filming) is a lovely inn which dates back to the last century. In 1955 it was the prize in a competition run by the now defunct "Daily Sketch" and the late Diana Dors presented it to the winner.

The Interpretation Centre is also certainly worth a visit with its colourful audio-visual show about the area. Its assistants are always on hand to talk about the history of Exeter, particularly its quayside, and provide a helpful, knowledgeable service.

New Bridges—Old River!

The bonded warehouses on the right of the photograph have been nightclubs for several decades so by night it is a place of great revelry (perhaps sometimes too boisterous as it has been known to spill over into the surrounding area) but by day it is hard to imagine a more tranquil scene. Coming from the right of the picture is a man-made watercourse, a leat, which was one of many that flowed over this flat part of land known as the Shilhay. Many of the leats were filled in as the area was changed from industrial to residential. The leats have been deleted!

Exeter Quay

On the right hand side of this photograph is a tall, elegant, green lamp post. On the opposite side of the Exe is another. This matching pair, painted in Exeter's official colour, were manufactured in Scotland by W Macfarlane and Co of Glasgow. There were originally six and they stood on an earlier Exe Bridge which was opened in 1905 but dismantled in 1973. In 1983 these lamps were restored and re-located here.

Exeter Quay Again!

The tall five-storey warehouses which dominate the scene were built by R.S. Cornish and Hoopers around about 1834. Today they perform the task of accommodating display areas for the Maritime Museum and also house a number of art and craft gift shops. There is also an unusual pub—"The Waterfront". This has proved to be a most popular venue specially on a fine summer's day or evening when the quay and riverside area comes alive.

Who Pays The Ferryman?

It may seem strange to have a ferry so close to a bridge over the Exe but the bridge is relatively new whereas crossing the river in this fashion goes back to 1750. Long ago, when the River Exe was tidal, it was possible to cross the river at this point by using a series of stepping stones. However, when a weir was created downstream it had the effect of ponding back the water thereby deepening it and rendering it impossible to cross. The City Fathers, who had commissioned the project which involved the weir construction, were obliged to help out and as a result a ferry appeared here. It is known as Butt's Ferry, named after George Butt, not a former ferryman but a professional local man. He stepped in to object to the axing of the ferry when it was claimed to be a burden on the local ratepayers. Eventually the matter was resolved when the Maritime Museum undertook to maintain the service and this unusual form of transport is well in keeping with the Maritime Museum's watery themes.

Trew's Weir

John Trew was an engineer who came to Exeter from South Wales in the 1560s. He was employed to construct Exeter's first canal, a modest waterway less than 2 miles long, 16 feet wide and just 3 feet deep. The weir, otherwise known as St Leonard's Weir, was constructed to create a head of water for this canal. Later the site beside the weir was used for various mills producing such items as cotton and later paper. The area in the vicinity of the mill has undergone enormous changes in recent years and those folk who regularly stroll the well walked Weirfield Path can always expect to see an interesting, ever changing scene.

The Cathedral City

From almost every angle Exeter's Cathedral dominates the skyline and without any doubt it is the city's most impressive and important landmark. This overview shows many of the city centre roof tops and Princesshay can be clearly identified in the foreground. In the distance the Haldon Hills can be spied with Belvedere (Lawrence Castle) tower a familiar landmark on the horizon, reminding us that Exeter is set in the heart of some glorious countryside.

14

The Cathedral Green

Richard Hooker has the best seat in the Cathedral Green and it is here he sits, somewhat stone-faced, gazing back at the many hundreds of visitors that come and stare at him each week in the season! His contemplative expression is appropriate as Hooker was a deeply thoughtful man who turned his mind to spiritual matters.

Hooker was born in 1543, at Heavitree, which was then a separate village rather than an integral part of Exeter as it is now. His parents were not wealthy but when it was realised he was blessed with an able brain his parents were granted an annual pension which enabled Hooker to go to Corpus Christi College, Oxford. Each term, for the first three years, he had to walk there but eventually Bishop Jewel, his patron, lent him a horse. Although he had a brilliant career and mind he made a great mistake in his choice of wife, described by one great English biographer, Izaak Walton, as "an ill bred, bad-tempered girl, neither rich nor beautiful." However, despite this adversity, our great scholar managed to write his masterpiece entitled "Of the Laws of Ecclesiastical Polity" which was championed by some but castigated by others. Just five years later, whilst travelling from London to Gravesend, he contracted a fatal virus and died in 1600.

It would be interesting to know what such a pious and devout man like Richard Hooker would make of some of the proceedings which go on all around him on the Cathedral Green today!

Exeter Cathedral

The Great West Front, which has a distinctly warmer face when basking in the afternoon sunshine, was built between 1345 and 1380. The enormous North and South Towers, which cast such long shadows over the eastern end of the Cathedral Close, are more than eight centuries old.

Mol's Coffee House

Many visitors to Exeter enter the Cathedral precincts via the narrow Martin's Lane which takes them past the "Ship Inn", reputedly one of Sir Francis Drake's old haunts—in the literal sense for he is said to haunt this inn! Martin's Lane leads into this photograph on the left hand side between The Royal Clarence and the SPCK Bookshop. The former can claim the distinction of being the first establishment in England, in 1769, to use the word "hotel". The small church apparently pushed into the corner of the Cathedral Close is St Martin's and it is dedicated to a French bishop who became a saint. Next door is number 1 Cathedral Close, known as Mol's Coffee House, but is in fact a jewellers, a little gem of architecture none the less.

The Cathedral Close

The Cathedral close contains some high quality shops and some wonderful old institutions. It is also home for many of the Cathedral clergy. Number 10 is the official residence of the Bishop of Crediton whilst The Devon and Exeter Institute is at Number 7 in a building which was formerly the town house of the Courtenays, Earls of Devon. A walk along the cobbled Close leads to a gap in the City Wall which is spanned by an unusual wrought iron bridge sponsored by Mayor Burnet Patch in 1814. The bridge made it possible to walk along the City Walls in order to inspect for damage. This tour, which was done annually, was called the Muraltie walk.

Southernhay—Georgian Exeter

Exeter was the boom town of the South West during Georgian times and many imposing terraces and crescents of town houses appeared. Between 1789 and 1840 Exeter doubled in size and it was one of the largest provincial towns in England. Southernhay, which is now almost completely devoted to offices, was largely the work of an architect called Matthew Nosworthy. The wealth of the owners of these properties was founded on the wool trade, brewing and leather tanning. Banking and commerce were, and still are, important functions of Exeter.

Far left is the most prominent feature of Exeter's High Street, the Guildhall. Nobody is certain of its date of origin, though the first concrete reference to it was a deed of gift about the year 1160 and the highly distinctive porticoed Elizabethan front was added between 1593-96. The Guildhall has served many purposes down through the years; the front cellar was used for holding prisoners until 1571 and the old provost court acted as a women's prison from 1472. In the seventeenth century better class prisoners were held in the Mayor's parlour! The outer hall housed all the city's fire appliances until 1835 and the room to the left of the entrance was used as a police station in Victorian times. The most important past use of the Guildhall was that of a court of justice with various courts being held there with crimes both great and small being tried.

The next photograph (on the same page) is a view of the newer half of the High Street, and on this page is a view of the Odeon Cinema in Sidwell Street, taken from the floral roundabout which is nearby.

Exeter in Bloom

There are many churches in and around the centre of Exeter and a visit to each would prove quite a pilgrimage. This is St Stephen's which has its entrance on the High Street. It is often used on Saturday mornings for charity events and is seen here photographed from the glamorous surroundings of the public conveniences in Catherine Street! A church was founded here before the coming of the Normans but after their arrival seems to have fallen into disuse as a place of worship and was used as a stable. Things were little improved in 1657 when troops were billeted here. However, at the Restoration the parishioners set about repairing it and better times seemed in prospect. Alas the inside of the church was gutted by fire and work had to begin all over again.

The present building thus dates from about 1664 and since then it seems to have endured everything which has been thrown at it including German bombs. The area immediately surrounding the church was heavily bombed and very few buildings were left standing. St Stephen's has a low arch, St Stephen's Bow, which leads through to the High Street.

Opposite (far left) is the High Street where it has a junction with Queen Street. The floral baskets, wide pavement and the reduced traffic flow help to make it a more attractive shopping area than it was in the past when an accidental foot off the pavement often threatened the survival of pedestrians.

The right hand picture on the opposite page is of Princesshay which was opened by the Queen when she was Princess Elizabeth, on October 21 1949.

The Underground Passages

There are certain things visitors to Exeter will do which local citizens probably never get round to trying. The most common of these 'oversights' are doing a tour of the entire city wall in one excursion and going down the underground passages. Having been a guide here, in my youth, I certainly found that a huge proportion of visitors to these medieval water passages or conduits were from outside of Devon. Anyone who makes the effort will see strange underground channels which once brought water into the city from powerful springs located outside the nearby East Gate. Although low in places, they are not at all stuffy and are well lit. This view shows one of the lowest passages, less than a yard high, more or less below the entrance to Boots in the High Street.

Volcanic Exeter

The floral theme of Exeter continues as wherever you go in the City you will be confronted by displays of vegetation, flowers or attractive trees. Just an Olympic athlete's stone throw from the City Centre is Rougemont Gardens which, until early this century, was originally the garden of a private dwelling. Sited on the side of an ancient volcanic outcrop, hence the name, it is a peaceful park divided by the City Wall from Northernhay Park, with access through a narrow arched thoroughfare. By contrast, the latter is believed to be one of the oldest laid out parks or "pleasure walks" in England, laid out in 1612!

Exeter Prison

A good view is to be had from the elevated plateau of Northernhay Park towards the hilly area to the north of Exeter. In Roman times there would have been a large forest stretching northwards as far as the eye could see. This wood was called Duryard and meant "Deer Wood". It was a hunting ground and an excellent source of timber and fuel. Today the University's campus occupies a large proportion of this land. The forbidding building in the foreground is Exeter Prison. There were nearly 80 executions carried out there between 1794 and 1877. Crowds would gather on the slopes of Northernhay in order to witness the public executions which took place in the dip beneath the prison.

Exeter University

Exeter University was established in 1956 and since then many thousands of students from all over the globe have studied here. To accommodate the demand, the campus has grown and spread across the hills. Much landscaping has gone on in and around the grounds to ensure that the setting has remained an attractive one. The Taddiford Brook rises on the University site and by a series of barriers has been ponded back to create scenes like this. The ever popular Northcott Theatre can be seen in the distance.

The Maritime Museum

The Maritime Museum is one of Exeter's main tourist attractions and apart from occupying most of Exeter Quay also utilises the Canal Basin where there is ample free car parking. This is a unique collection of craft gathered from all over the world by the International Sailing Craft Association (ISCA). Included are dhows, coracles, reed-boats, tugs and visitors are encouraged to touch, pull or push most of the operating controls on vessels. Exeter's present canal reached the size it is today in 1827 and this Basin was added, by the celebrated engineer James Green, in 1830. The Maritime Museum also occupies some of the former warehouses.

The Double Locks

The Exeter Canal is just over 5 miles long and it is possible to walk the entire length from the Canal Basin to the Turf Hotel where the canal enters the Exe Estuary. This is the "Double Locks" just over a mile south of the Basin. It is a most popular venue as a pub and on fine summer evenings is packed with mainly young people who sit outside in the large gardens. The hotel was built of clinkers, small bricks which were brought back as ballast from Holland in the days when Exeter did much trade with that part of Europe.

The Exeter Canal

This evening sunset was taken from the swing bridge over the Exeter Canal at the Exeter by-pass. The best way to escape from the incessant sound of traffic is to walk the towpaths. From here it is about half a mile north to the "Double Locks" or about two and a half miles south to the Turf Hotel. In each case the west bank affords an easier passage underfoot. For those who like variety it is possible to walk along the canal, for just over a mile, and then take a passenger ferry across to Topsham where there are 14 pubs—say no more!

Topsham

Topsham is part of Exeter but no self respecting local would go out of his or her way to stress the point. The town has an olde worlde charm all of its own and is well worth exploring. Its museum gives a marvellous impression of the town's heyday when it was a thriving port with many allied maritime pursuits taking place. Today its waterfront has been largely redeveloped but there are a few places left where a comfortable, sheltered seat can be found to enjoy the view across the Exe Estuary towards the Haldon Hills.

And It's Goodnight From Me . . .

for the real thing—a real tonic after a hectic day.

A lovely time to visit the Exe Estuary is as sunset approaches. A photograph like this can convey the mood of such a serene scene but there is no substitute

I hope you have enjoyed this brief look at the City of Exeter in a personal selection of photographs which have been taken more for their colourful appearance than for their historic significance. For further, more detailed, light-hearted reading may I suggest "The Great Little Exeter Book" and "The Lost City of Exeter".